This book is dedicated to our children, our guests, and locals who all love living in and exploring the Cayman Islands.

Explore Grand Cayman, Cayman Brac, and Little Cayman!

It's a beautiful day to be in the Cayman Islands!

The sun is warm and bright.

There are so many things to see and do in all three islands.
Time to explore them!

We can visit the Grounds in Savannah with our family.

Let's get some local fruit like mangoes, guineps, or even a star fruit.
Let's ask which fruit is ripe, juicy, and ready to eat.

We can visit with a Caymanian lady who makes hats and bags
from the palms of our wonderful Silver Thatch.

Let's get some pepper jelly for a friend, or maybe some fresh cold
coconut water as a tasty treat!

Let's go on the boat with Captain Ebanks and explore the beautiful ocean with our family and friends.

We can snorkel the coral reefs, look into the clear blue water, and watch the angelfish, the parrotfish, and the squirrelfish swimming in and around the coral.

We can stop at Starfish Point and see the beautiful bright orange starfish just beneath the surface of the ocean.

We can swim with the stingrays at Stingray City, where they live. It's not very deep, so we can even stand and splash in the water.

We are very lucky! Since it's conch season now, we can take a few pretty conch shells from the ocean and watch the Captain make marinated conch for our lunch!

Let's visit the Mission House, or Pedro's Castle, in Bodden Town.

There is so much to see and history to learn!

We can talk to the people and find out many things.

Did you know that many fathers in Cayman were fishermen?

They went out on big boats for many months to catch fish so they could take care of their families.

Did you know that families used to make their homes from materials called 'wattle' and 'daub'?

These homes were sturdy and strong.

Did you know that children went exploring to find hermit crabs?

They drew a circle in the sand, placed the crabs together in the middle, and watched the crabs crawl out of the circle.

This was a crab race, and it was very fun to play!

A long time ago, there were so many turtles in the sea that the Cayman Islands used to be called 'Las Tortugas'.

'Las Tortugas' is Spanish. It means 'The Turtles' in English.

Let's visit the turtles at the Cayman Turtle Farm in West Bay.

We can find turtles of all different sizes.

Turtle eggs are buried under the sand and are waiting to hatch.

Baby turtles are swimming together, and if you are careful, you may even get to hold one!

The big turtles swim in the water and rest on the sand.

Almost every year, a hundred sea turtles are released into our beautiful ocean.

It's amazing to watch these turtles crawl to the ocean. They leave turtle tracks called 'Batabano' and then swim in the open waters of our Caribbean Sea!

Let's explore North Side.

Remember to bring your camera when we visit the Botanical Park!

This is a wonderful place to see beautiful plants, trees, and flowers.

We can explore, searching for our National flower, the Banana Orchid.

There is a peaceful lake, where birds rest and take cool sips of water.

Many different kinds of butterflies like to live in the park. The birds and butterflies love all the flowers.

We can walk through the park. We will see our native Blue Iguanas, hear the birds chirping and see many different types of plants and cacti.

Let's walk through George Town.

It's Pirates' Week and there is a pirates' parade.

There is a pirates' landing, and many people will be dressed in costumes.

There will be pirates and wenches who will parade through the streets.

We can watch them as they walk by, and if they stop, maybe we will get a doubloon or a necklace made of beads!

We can see all the beautiful floats that pass by in the parade.

There will be steel pan music being played, bright colours of red, black, and gold and delicious local dishes, like conch stew, fried plantain, with rice and beans to eat.

Let's go to a fish shack in East End.

There's a great fish shack on the beach that sells food.

We will see so many locals and visitors.

We can smile and say 'Hello!' to everyone.

We can get some fresh fried fish, with breadfruit and fritters.

Maybe they will even have some freshly made tamarind juice to drink!

We can sit at one of the wooden tables on the beach while we eat and enjoy the salty ocean breeze, watching the waves gently roll onto the sand.

It's such a beautiful day to keep exploring!
Let's go to the airport and get on a Cayman Airways airplane.

We can fly to Cayman Brac!

Let's discover caves, like the Bat Cave, or Peter's Cave
to see all the different rock formations in the caves.

We can climb the Bluff. When we get to the top of
these limestone cliffs, we will be able to see the island
from up high and look at the beautiful ocean all around us.

Maybe we will even see a family of brown Booby birds.
The babies are fluffy and white.
When these birds grow up, their feathers change colours!

Keep looking up and find other birds, like the Cayman Parrot.

Let's look down and around on the ground to find a
Rock Iguana. Rock Iguanas are different from the famous
Blue Iguanas found in Grand Cayman.

There is one more island to visit.
It's the smallest of the three islands.
Let's go explore Little Cayman!

We can go fishing. Bring the rods, hooks, and bait!

We can lay under a palm tree in a hammock, or we can get binoculars to look for Owen Island.

Let's build sand castles high up to the sky and decorate them with beautiful sea shells, like limpets and cockle shells.

Then, get buried in the sand and turn your legs into a mermaid's tail!

Swim in the water with splashy toes at Point of Sand and blow lots of bubbles when you look down into the blue ocean.

It was a beautiful day, and we had so much fun exploring the Cayman Islands!

Let's watch the sun go down.

It's sinking down past the horizon. There's not a cloud in the sky.

Don't blink! Did you see the green flash?

Now the stars are coming out, the moon is in the sky, and the birds, fish, and iguanas are all asleep.

Good night, Cayman Islands!

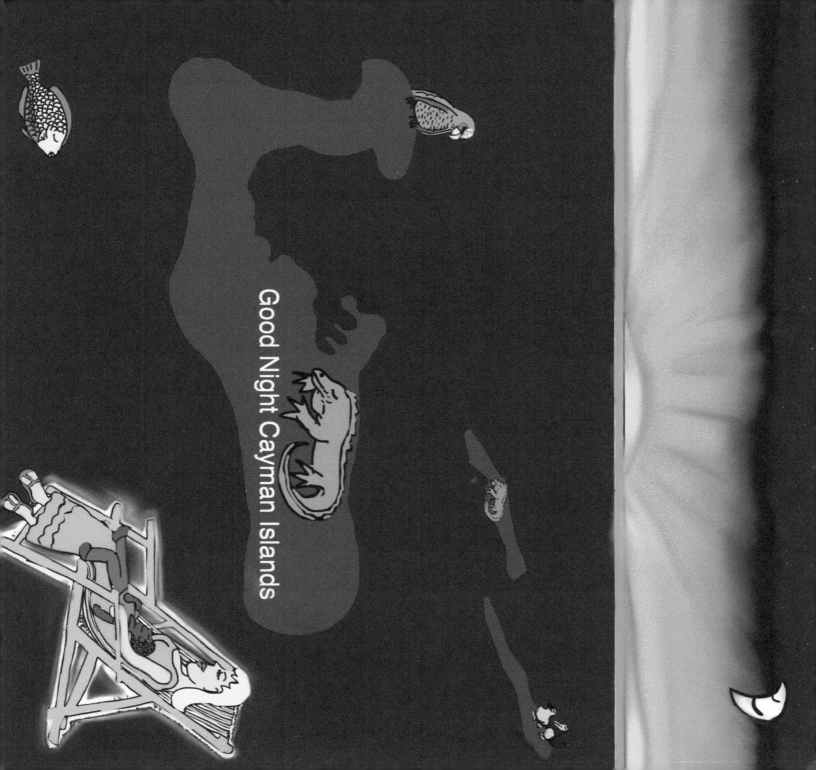

Good Night Cayman Islands

Let's Explore the Cayman Islands
Copyright © 2014 by Taura Ebanks

Acknowledgement

As someone who loves living and exploring all three of the Cayman Islands that I call home, a special thanks goes to these wonderful people:

My grandfather, Keith Rayner. His words of support for this book mean more than I can express.

Aleksander Valldejuli, the curious little explorer who loves searching for hermit crabs, flying on planes and is a wonderful reminder that having fun at every age is so very important!

Barbara and Ed at Book Nook in the Cayman Islands, two original and special people who have always encouraged me to read, learn, and discover as much as I can.

Special thanks to those family members and close friends who have inspired and reminded me to include all the best parts of our lives in this book.

CPSIA information can be obtained
at www.ICGtesting.com
Printed in the USA
LVHW020330230519
618830LV00024B/543/P

9 780692 240229